The Best Of
BEAR LAKE COUNTRY
A Rocky Mountain National Park
Insider's

Published By The Rocky M ...ATION

CONTENTS

THINGS TO KNOW BEFORE YOU GO

WEATHER WISDOM

 Weather in Rocky Mountain National Park is often unpredictable and sometimes extreme. Temperatures drop as elevation increases, so be prepared for chilly temperatures year-round, especially at higher elevations. Be sure to:

▲ Begin hikes early to assure a safe return before the onset of afternoon storms, which often bring dangerous lightning.

▲ Carry rain gear for protection against the brief, heavy rain common during summer storms.

▲ Bring layers of clothing to accommodate changing temperatures.

▲ Pack winter gear designed for cold and wind.

IF YOU LOVE THE WATER

 The Bear Lake region boasts the park's highest concentration of lakes, streams and waterfalls east of the Continental Divide. Please enjoy these destinations safely and responsibly. Remember to:

▲ Watch children closely.

▲ Be careful near streams and rivers. Rocks often are slippery. The water can be fast and powerful, and it's always cold.

▲ Know the fishing regulations. Angling is allowed in designated areas only, and a valid Colorado fishing license is required for adults.

PROTECT OUR PAST

To help assure that generations to come have the opportunity to understand the park's human history:

▲ Leave historical and archeological artifacts where you find them.

▲ Report any damage or vandalism to a park ranger.

▲ Respect private property.

WATCHING WILDLIFE

 Wildlife viewing is best at dawn and dusk in locations where different habitats – such as meadows and forests – meet. To help keep wildlife wild:

▲ Never feed wild animals. It's harmful to wildlife and illegal in national parks.

▲ Watch wildlife and take pictures from a distance. If the animal seems nervous or alters its behavior, you're too close. Wild animals may bite, kick or charge without warning.

ESSENTIALS

▲ Plenty of water
▲ Nutritious snacks
▲ Sturdy walking shoes
▲ Rain gear
▲ Warm sweater or jacket
▲ Clothing layers
▲ Gloves and hat
▲ Sunglasses and sunscreen
▲ First-aid kit
▲ Flashlight
▲ Waterproof matches
▲ Pocket knife
▲ Whistle
▲ Trail guide
▲ Topographical map and compass

THINK AHEAD

Restroom facilities in the backcountry are limited. Use restrooms at the trailheads.

Kings crown. Duane B. Squires

Introduction

E ach summer morning, a fortunate few pass through one of Rocky Mountain National Park's entrance stations on their way to work.

These commuters are park rangers, naturalists whose job descriptions include sharing their knowledge of Rocky Mountain's jaw-dropping landscapes, plants, animals and human history with visitors. Their "office" is somewhere along Bear Lake Road, perhaps in the Moraine Park Museum, the information kiosk at Bear Lake or out on a hiking trail.

In *The Best Of Bear Lake Country*, park ranger/naturalists offer insights into their favorite destinations along and above Bear Lake Road, which winds 9 scenic miles from Beaver Meadows to Bear Lake. Like most of Rocky Mountain National Park, this popular region welcomes one and all – sightseers, hikers, climbers, campers, backpackers, wildlife watchers, photographers, horseback riders, picnickers, fishermen, cross-country skiers, snowshoers and many others – to a spectacular, family-friendly wilderness.

In the Bear Lake area, visitors find jewel-like lakes with breathtaking backdrops, ice-cold, crystal-clear streams that cascade down spectacular waterfalls, great forests of pine, spruce, fir and aspen, soar-

Bear Lake Road. James Frank

ing mountain summits, amazing wildlife, colorful plant life and a few remnants of a surprisingly rich human history.

This is some office, to be sure. Pick a destination suited to your level of conditioning. Equip yourself with the proper maps, guides and gear, and go see for yourself.

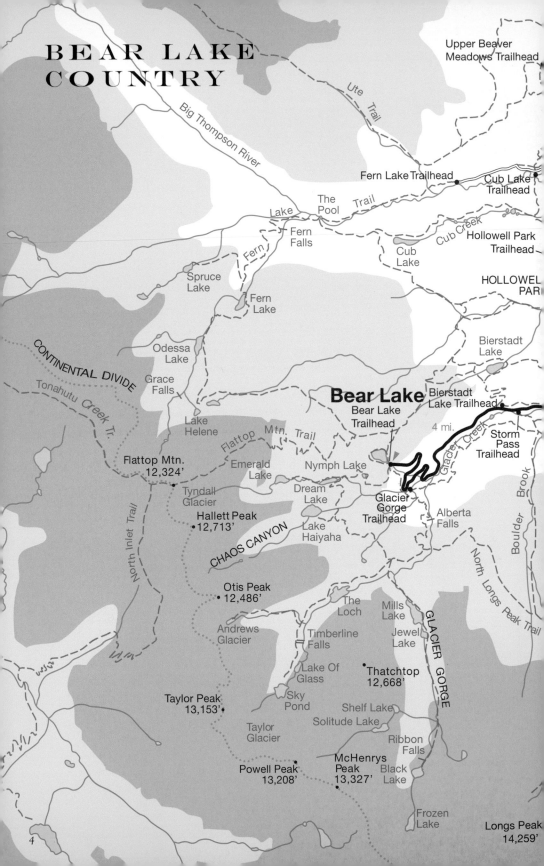

BEAR LAKE COUNTRY

Upper Beaver Meadows Trailhead

Ute Trail

Big Thompson River

Fern Lake Trailhead

Cub Lake Trailhead

Cub Creek

Hollowell Park Trailhead

The Pool

Lake Trail

Fern Falls

Cub Lake

HOLLOWELL PAR

Spruce Lake

Fern

Fern Lake

CONTINENTAL DIVIDE

Tonahutu Creek Tr.

Odessa Lake

Grace Falls

Bierstadt Lake

Bear Lake

Bierstadt Lake Trailhead

Bear Lake Trailhead

4 mi.

Lake Helene

Flattop Mtn. Trail

Glacier Creek

Storm Pass Trailhead

Flattop Mtn. 12,324'

Emerald Lake

Nymph Lake

Boulder Brook

Tyndall Glacier

Dream Lake

Glacier Gorge Trailhead

Alberta Falls

North Inlet Trail

Hallett Peak • 12,713'

CHAOS CANYON

Lake Haiyaha

North Longs Peak Trail

Otis Peak • 12,486'

The Loch

Mills Lake

Andrews Glacier

Timberline Falls

Jewel Lake

GLACIER GORGE

Lake Of Glass

Taylor Peak 13,153'

Thatchtop 12,668'

Sky Pond

Shelf Lake

Solitude Lake

Taylor Glacier

Ribbon Falls

Powell Peak 13,208'

McHenrys Peak 13,327'

Black Lake

Frozen Lake

Longs Peak 14,259'

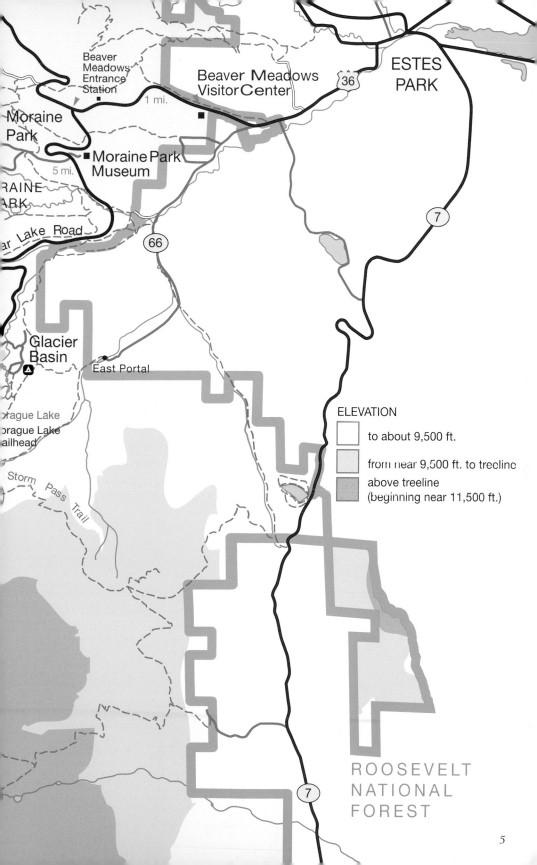

Beaver Meadows
Entrance Station

1 mi.

Beaver Meadows
Visitor Center

36

ESTES
PARK

Moraine
Park

5 mi.

Moraine Park
Museum

RAINE
RK

ar Lake Road

66

7

Glacier
Basin

East Portal

rague Lake

rague Lake
ailhead

Storm   Pass   Trail

ELEVATION

to about 9,500 ft.

from near 9,500 ft. to treeline

above treeline
(beginning near 11,500 ft.)

ROOSEVELT
NATIONAL
FOREST

7

5

Hallett Peak reflected in Bear Lake. James Frank

INSIDER'S PICK

Bear Lake

Access: Bear Lake Trailhead
Distance one-way: 0.6 miles (around lake, wheelchair accessible with assistance)
Access elevation: 9,475 feet
Destination elevation: 9,475 feet

Let's start with the obvious. On many summer days, Bear Lake may be the busiest place in Rocky Mountain National Park.

Visitors flock to this shimmering subalpine lake because it offers easy year-round access to splendid mountain scenery and serves as a hiking hub to many of Rocky Mountain National Park's premier backcountry destinations. Great granite peaks of the Continental Divide, including Longs Peak, Hallett Peak and Flattop Mountain, tower above the waters of a lake that is tucked snugly into dense forests of evergreen and aspen. The big picture is mighty impressive, but this lake that was dug and dammed by Ice Age glaciers invites closer scrutiny.

Encircling Bear Lake is the 0.6-mile Bear Lake Nature Trail. Thirty signed stops along the pathway are detailed in the *Bear Lake Nature Trail* guidebook available at the trailhead and in bookstores around the park. The stops offer fascinating insights into the lake area's scenery, geology, wildlife, plant life and human history (some local pathways were traveled by Native Americans 6,000 years ago).

> **Inside Scoop:** "The parking lot usually fills by **9 a.m.** in the summertime. Visit after 4 p.m., when the crowds are gone, or take the shuttle from **Park**-and-Ride."

Alberta Falls. James Frank

Sprague Lake. James Frank

Alberta Falls

Access: Glacier Gorge Trailhead   **Distance one-way:** 0.9 miles
Access elevation: 9,180 feet   **Destination elevation:** 9,400 feet

Alberta Falls is one of the park's most popular waterfalls. Many visitors swear it's also one of the prettiest. Water thunders down this impressive Glacier Gorge drop-off even during the driest years, sending a cooling spray toward appreciative hikers on warm summer days.

Gazing at Alberta – and all other park waterfalls – can be as mesmerizing as staring into a nighttime campfire. No less enjoyable is the hike in. The trail makes several stream crossings as it travels uphill through forests of pine, spruce, fir and aspen. Exceptional views abound along a path that is popular year-round.

In the spring, visitors marvel as Glacier Creek, swollen with snowmelt, tumbles down Alberta Falls, a favorite autumn destination for hikers enjoying the turning-leaf color displays put on by the abundant groves of aspen. Come winter, the frozen waterfall attracts cross-country skiers and snowshoers.

> **Inside Scoop:** "Graffiti scars many of the beautiful aspen trunks along this well-used trail. Please resist any temptation to further damage these trees."

Sprague Lake

Access: Sprague Lake Trailhead   **Distance one-way:** 0.5 miles (around lake, wheelchair accessi
Access elevation: 8,710 feet   **Destination elevation:** 8,710 feet

The ideal spot for families, visitors in wheelchairs and newcomers seeking to acclimate to the high-altitude environment, Sprague Lake always has been a welcoming place. Surrounded by a wheelchair-accessible trail offering drop-dead Continental Divide scenery, Sprague Lake was built in the early 20th century to provide trout fishing for guests at a resort owned by local pioneer Abner E. Sprague. The lakeside retreat is long gone, but the area still offers visitors an easy introduction to Rocky Mountain National Park's myriad natural wonders.

The hard-packed, half-mile trail around the lake follows level terrain. The views of Hallett Peak and its neighboring summits are exceptional, particularly from the east shoreline. Sprague Lake is family-friendly, offering opportunities for young and old to enjoy picnics on strategically placed benches and examinations of the lake's plant, animal and insect life. Especially entertaining are the ducks, which paddle around the lake with their young in tow and bob upside down for meals. Please don't share lunch or snacks with them.

> **Inside Scoop:** "The fishing at Sprague Lake can be good, but the water is cold. The best way to fish there is with a belly boat or waders."

Odessa Lake

Access: Bear Lake Trailhead
Distance one-way: 4.0 miles
Access elevation: 9,475 feet
Destination elevation: 10,020 feet

It's a simple rule. As hiking distances increase, crowds decrease. A sublime spot located in one of the park's most spectacular settings, Odessa Lake is a powerful lure, but its relative isolation assures a near-wilderness experience.

Hikers depart for Odessa Lake from both the Fern Lake and Bear Lake trailheads. Many begin at one access point and exit at the other, taking advantage of the park's free seasonal shuttle bus for a ride to or from their vehicles. The vote here is to hike from Bear Lake to Odessa along a trail that is shorter than the footpath from the Fern Lake Trailhead and involves less elevation gain.

After enjoying invigorating exercise, spectacular scenery and forests of aspen, pine, spruce and fir during an almost 1,200-foot ascent to the trek's high point, Odessa Lake-bound hikers are treated to vistas of their destination nestled in the trees hundreds of feet below. Head on down. Odessa Lake has it all: azure water rimmed by a subalpine forest, mountains towering above, a sandy little beach and with a little luck, solitude, splendid solitude.

Inside Scoop: "Odessa Lake supports a population of greenback cutthroat trout, once almost extinct in the park. Fishing at the lake is catch-and-release only."

Odessa Lake. James Frank

Nymph Lake

Access: Bear Lake Trailhead
Distance one-way: 0.5 miles
Access elevation: 9,475 feet
Destination elevation: 9,700 feet

Every summer, the water at this little beauty (a pleasant half-mile hike from the Bear Lake Trailhead on a paved path) is flecked with the bright-yellow blooms of pond lilies. Rich in organic sediments that encourage the growth of plant life, Nymph Lake also affords soaring views of Flattop Mountain, Hallett Peak, Longs Peak and the Keyboard of the Winds. The lake's proximity to Bear Lake virtually assures that you'll never be alone. Come early or late to avoid the crowds.

Inside Scoop: "Sunrise at Nymph Lake often reveals Hallett Peak awash in a spectacular orange-and-pink optical phenomenon called alpenglow."

Nymph Lake. James Frank

Dream Lake. James Frank

Dream Lake

Access: Bear Lake Trailhead
Distance one-way: 1.1 miles
Access elevation: 9,475 feet
Destination elevation: 9,900 feet

This lake lives up to its name. Hallett Peak and Flattop Mountain, two grand summits in the Bear Lake view, are closer and even more impressive at Dream Lake. Ancient limber pines frame dream-like views of the two peaks and what remains of Tyndall Glacier, which long ago scoured out the gorge below. Large rocks along the shoreline of this long, narrow lake invite hikers who have walked in on the relatively easy trail to find a pleasant place to rest, enjoy a picnic ... even dream a little.

> **Inside Scoop:** "The aggressive, overweight, unhealthy ground squirrels and chipmunks at Dream Lake have been fed by careless hikers. Never, ever feed wildlife."

Emerald Lake

Access: Bear Lake Trailhead
Distance one-way: 1.8 miles
Access elevation: 9,475 feet
Destination elevation: 10,080 feet

Emerald Lake truly is a jewel. Less than a mile beyond Dream Lake and often reflecting the face of Hallett Peak, the lake has a greenish cast that justifies its name. Like many lakes found in glacially scoured, steep-walled mountain basins called cirques, Emerald does not support a fish population. However, this high-elevation lake fed by Tyndall Glacier makes up for its angling

shortcomings by providing clear water glistening in the sunshine, Continental Divide scenery and early-morning and late-day solitude.

> **Inside Scoop:** "Walk to the far end of the lake (not many people do). Sit and enjoy the waterfall, peace, serenity and incredible beauty."

Lake Haiyaha

Access: Bear Lake Trailhead
Distance one-way: 2.2 miles
Access elevation: 9,475 feet
Destination elevation: 10,220 feet

Haiyaha is different. Perhaps it's the rugged, boulder-strewn shoreline, which requires that hikers exploring the lakeshore exercise special caution. Lake Haiyaha is situated in the lower portion of a rocky ravine aptly named Chaos Canyon. Haiyaha and its Hallett Peak vistas await about a mile up the trail after a respite at Dream Lake.

> **Inside Scoop:** "The Grandma Tree, a large, centuries-old limber pine hikers see upon their arrival at Lake Haiyaha, is one of the oldest trees in the park."

Emerald Lake. James Frank

The Loch

Access: Glacier Gorge Trailhead
Distance one-way: 3.1 miles
Access elevation: 9,180 feet
Destination elevation: 10,180 feet

Which is more beautiful: Mills Lake or The Loch? Take your pick. Both are spectacular bodies of water set in long valleys carved by glaciers. Many hikers let their conditioning and energy levels determine which trail to follow. The Loch is a quarter mile farther in and 240 feet higher in elevation.

Visitors marvel when water and air temperatures combine to create an eerie fog that creeps across The Loch in late summer and early fall. Picnics enjoyed on lakeside rocks likely will draw the attention of Clark's nutcrackers, camp-robbing jays that are supposed to be eating the seeds of limber pinecones. Please don't feed them when they come calling.

Inside Scoop: "'Those people must be crazy.' That's often muttered by hikers watching daring technical climbers creep across the Cathedral Wall above The Loch."

The Loch. David Halpern

Veteran park hikers rank Timberline Falls among the park's loveliest. The waters of Icy Brook cascading more than 250 feet over these tiered cliffs are seen on the final approach to the falls, where hikers pause to enjoy lush, verdant subalpine scenery at its best.

Inside Scoop: "The distinctive sound of marmots whistling their warning calls often is heard in the meadow below Timberline Falls."

Timberline Falls

Access: Glacier Gorge Trailhead
Distance one-way: 4.0 miles
Access elevation: 9,180 feet
Destination elevation: 10,450 feet

Sky Pond

Access: Glacier Gorge Trailhead
Distance one-way: 4.6 miles
Access elevation: 9,180 feet
Destination elevation: 10,900 feet

After enjoying their visit to Timberline Falls, hardy hikers continue past starkly beautiful Lake of Glass to Sky Pond. Taylor Glacier scoured out this small lake thousands of years ago. The glacier's modest remnant still occupies the ridge between Powell and Taylor peaks, Continental Divide summits that comprise much of Sky Pond's exceptional backdrop.

This is high and rugged country where the last stunted tree growth clings to life before giving way to the vast alpine tundra, the land above the trees. After working hard to reach this remote destination, hikers thrill to the grand vistas commonplace on the walk back down to the trailhead.

Inside Scoop: "Be careful when making the steep ascent along the west side of Timberline Falls. The rocks are dangerously slick when icy, snowy or wet."

Timberline Falls. James Frank

11

Mills Lake

Access: Glacier Gorge Trailhead
Distance one-way: 2.8 miles
Access elevation: 9,180 feet
Destination elevation: 9,940 feet

This gorgeous lake was named in honor of Enos A. Mills, a local writer-naturalist who campaigned tirelessly for Rocky Mountain National Park's preservation prior to its establishment in 1915. A long, narrow lake nestled in a scenic glacial valley, Mills Lake is nearly surrounded by great mountains, notably Longs Peak, the adjacent Keyboard of the Winds, Pagoda Mountain and Chiefs Head Peak.

Most hikers arrive in the summer, when Mills Lake sparkles in the bright sunshine. In the fall, when the aspen leaves are aglow and clouds often shroud the peaks above, undergrowth contributes red and orange hues to the stunning Mills Lake landscape. Many families enjoy this destination hailed as one of the park's most picturesque spots. That's probably what Enos Mills and his fellow visionaries had in mind when they promoted the establishment of Rocky Mountain National Park.

> **Inside Scoop:** "Mills Lake has wonderful flat rocks where hikers can spread out, enjoy a picnic lunch and soak up some sun."

Black Lake. James Frank

Black Lake

Access: Glacier Gorge Trailhead
Distance one-way: 5.0 miles
Access elevation: 9,180 feet
Destination elevation: 10,620 feet

This is the real deal, the high, wild and rugged Rocky Mountains. Reached soon after a climb along beautiful Ribbon Falls, Black Lake rests at the foot of Continental Divide peaks that tower above Glacier Gorge. Hikers pondering the very difficult ascent of 13,327-foot McHenrys Peak might entertain second thoughts while taking in the overwhelming view of the mountain from Black Lake. Be warned that the higher portions of the trail to the lake may be snow-covered and slippery well into summer as Black Lake sheds its winter ice.

> **Inside Scoop:** "At Black Lake, walk south to the grassy meadow. It's a great picnic spot with beautiful views of McHenrys Peak."

Mills Lake. David Halpern

Cub Lake. David Halpern

Bierstadt Lake

Access: Bierstadt Lake Trailhead
Distance one-way: 1.4 miles
Access elevation: 8,850 feet
Destination elevation: 9,416 feet

Bierstadt Lake sits atop a forested moraine, a ridge composed of material left behind thousands of years ago by receding glaciers. It is a shallow lake that holds melting snow and rainwater – no streams flow in or out. Hikers making this steep climb enjoy classic views of the Continental Divide from the northeast side of the lake, and on calm days, the peaks are reflected in the water.

Also easily accessed from Bear Lake, Bierstadt Lake is a good place to search for aquatic life. There are no fish in the lake, but sharp-eyed observers – maybe the kids – might spot interesting insects in the water or a tiger salamander nearby. Watch out for aggressive ducks that have been known to steal an unsuspecting hiker's lunch.

> **Inside Scoop:** "If the water's not too high, hikers hang out at a small beach on Bierstadt's east shoreline."

Cub Lake

Access: Cub Lake Trailhead
Distance one-way: 2.3 miles
Access elevation: 8,080 feet
Destination elevation: 8,620 feet

Like Nymph Lake, Cub Lake is renowned for its pond lilies and their yellow flowers. But the hike to this lower-elevation (by park standards) lake offers experiences that are unique.

The trail starts out with a Big Thompson River crossing before skirting the western portion of Moraine Park, a vast glacial valley often visited by grazing elk. Flowers abound in the spring and summer, and the fall colors – both aspen and undergrowth – are exceptional. Hikers follow running water past ponds dammed by beavers. Keep an eye out for tracks in the mud and freshly gnawed trees. Cub Lake itself is pretty, peaceful and a great place to relax with family or friends.

> **Inside Scoop:** "This trail is a favorite among park visitors acclimating to the elevation or shaping up for more rigorous hikes ahead."

Fern Lake. James Frank

Fern Falls

Access: Fern Lake Trailhead
   (free seasonal shuttle stop 0.8 miles)
Distance one-way: 2.7 miles
Access elevation: 8,155 feet
Destination elevation: 8,800 feet

Fern Falls thunders through a forest of Engelmann spruce and subalpine fir. Its sound is a wilderness symphony that builds to a crescendo as hikers approach. The tree- and rock-strewn waterfall is the second notable stream feature seen along this portion of the Fern Lake Trail. Before reaching the falls, hikers encounter The Pool, an impressive granite basin filled by the rushing Big Thompson River. On hot days, park visitors heading to and from destinations beyond welcome the cool mist from Fern Falls.

> **Inside Scoop:** "Fern Falls is especially scenic early and late in the season when the water is partially frozen."

Fern Lake

Access: Fern Lake Trailhead
   (free seasonal shuttle stop 0.8 miles)
Distance one-way: 3.8 miles
Access elevation: 8,155 feet
Destination elevation: 9,530 feet

On a perfect summer day, Fern Lake is the perfect place to be. After crossing the clear stream flowing through the lake's outlet, hikers stand beside one of Rocky Mountain National Park's most beautiful bodies of water. Towering above is the Little Matterhorn, and the stunning vistas extend high into Odessa Gorge. Standing guard on the forested lakeshore is a rustic ranger patrol cabin. People and nature long have met at Fern Lake, once the site of a popular guest lodge, one of the few without a parking lot.

> **Inside Scoop:** "The trailhead's parking area fills early each summer morning. Ride the shuttle and avoid the frustration of an often unsuccessful search for a space."

Shelf Lake, west of the trail through Glacier Gorge. Glenn Randall

YELLOW-BELLIED MARMOT
Marmota flaviventris
Habitat: Rock piles

11,500 FEET

STELLER'S JAY
Cyanocitta stelleri
Habitat: Coniferous forests

LONG-TAILED WEASEL
Mustela frenata
Habitat: All habitats, especially rocky, brushy areas

CLARK'S NUTCRACKER
Nucifraga columbiana
Habitat: Coniferous forests

GOLDEN-MANTLED GROUND SQUIRREL
Spermophilus lateralis
Habitat: Rocky areas at forest edges

COYOTE
Canis latrans
Habitat: All habitats

MOUNTAIN LION
Felis concolor
Habitat: Rocky canyons, cliffs

PIKA
Ochotona princeps
Habitat: Rock piles

WHITE-TAILED PTARMIGAN
Lagopus leucurus
Habitat: Willows, rock outcrops

CHICKAREE (Red Squirrel)
Tamiasciurus hudsonicus
Habitat: Coniferous forests

SNOWSHOE HARE
Lepus americanus
Habitat: Brushy areas in forests

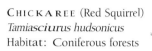

GRAY JAY
Perisoreus canadensis
Habitat: Coniferous forests

LEAST CHIPMUNK
Tamias minimus
Habitat: Coniferous forest
edges and openings

BLACK BEAR
Ursus americanus
Habitat: Forests

BLACK-BILLED MAGPIE
Pica pica
Habitat: Open forests

MULE DEER
Odocoileus hemionus
Habitat: All habitats

ELK
Cervus elaphus
Habitat: Meadows, forest edges

(From right) Flattop Mountain, Hallett and Otis peaks. Glenn Randall

INSIDER'S PICK

Flattop Mountain

Access: Bear Lake Trailhead
Distance one-way: 4.4 miles
Access elevation: 9,475 feet
Destination elevation: 12,324 feet

Hikers who succumb to the irresistible allure of standing atop Rocky Mountain National Park's awe-inspiring peaks inevitably find themselves on the summit of Flattop Mountain. Many climb the mountain en route to nearby peaks or hiking destinations west of the Continental Divide. Flattop itself, however, is a most satisfying summit.

The Flattop Mountain Trail winds uphill through blooming summer wildflowers, groves of aspen and forests of pine, spruce and fir. The subalpine evergreens become smaller, windswept and weather-beaten as treeline and the alpine tundra approach. While hiking in the treeless alpine world above 11,000 feet, keep an eye out for tundra wildlife such as marmots, pikas and ptarmigans.

Magnificent scenery abounds from start to finish, including perspectives of Dream and Emerald lakes from high above. The views from the massive summit of Flattop Mountain are extravagant, encompassing the Bear Lake Road corridor, the Continental Divide, Odessa Gorge and Grand Lake.

> **Inside Scoop:** "Thousands of years ago, Native American hunters crossed Flattop Mountain on their travels across the Continental Divide."

Flattop Mountain Trail. James Frank

Hallett Peak

Access: Bear Lake Trailhead
Distance one-way: 5.0 miles
Access elevation: 9,475 feet
Destination elevation: 12,713 feet

Hallett Peak stands shoulder-to-shoulder with Flattop Mountain, commanding the attention of the thousands of park visitors who take in the famed Bear Lake views each year. A 0.6-mile walk down from Flattop past the head of Tyndall Glacier and up a fairly steep slope, the "sharpest peak in the Front Range" (as one climber referred to Hallett Peak in 1887) joins Longs Peak atop the park's list of signature summits.

Don't expect to spend much time alone on Hallett — it's a popular climb. Consider this rewarding experience a social outing, and enjoy the company. There are wilder peaks to be climbed in that breathtaking panorama viewed from the summit.

Taylor Peak. James Frank

Inside Scoop: "The views from Hallett Peak are even more spectacular than the vistas seen from Flattop."

Otis Peak

Access: Bear Lake Trailhead
Distance one-way: 6.0 miles
Access elevation: 9,475 feet
Destination elevation: 12,486 feet

Lacking a clear trail and located between the more imposing summits of Hallett and Taylor peaks, Otis Peak sometimes gets little respect. Many hikers come and go in a hurry during a classic park "peak bagging" excursion that begins atop Flattop Mountain. Please give Otis its due. Situated slightly east of the Continental Divide, this massive mountain offers terrific scenery and the satisfaction of another great summit ascended.

Inside Scoop: "Dr. Edward Otis hardly let the naming of a mountain in his honor go to his head: 'Under what circumstances my name was given to the peak I do not remember.'"

Taylor Peak

Access: Bear Lake Trailhead
Distance one-way: 7.1 miles
Access elevation: 9,475 feet
Destination elevation: 13,153 feet

The hike to Taylor Peak attracts in-shape mountaineers, including hardy peak baggers who summit Flattop, Hallett and Otis along the way. After trekking across the high Continental Divide ridge, hikers negotiate steep, rocky terrain leading to the top of Taylor, which offers striking scenery downward to The Loch and north, south and west to Rocky Mountain ranges near and far. Hikers relaxing on Taylor's summit also may experience something not always found at Bear Lake area hiking destinations: solitude, that increasingly rare commodity.

Inside Scoop: "Sliding down Andrews Glacier on the descent is tempting, but extremely dangerous because of possible crevasses, icy conditions and exposed rocks."

ALPINE AVENS
Acomastylis rossii ssp. *turbinata*

MOSS CAMPION
Silene acaulis ssp. *subacaulescens*

RYDBERGIA
Rydbergia grandiflora

HEARTLEAF ARNICA
Arnica cordifolia

COLORADO COLUMBINE
Aquilegia coerulea

TALL CHIMINGBELLS
Mertensia ciliata

SCARLET PAINTBRUSH
Castilleja miniata

MOUNTAIN HAREBELL
Campanula rotundifolia

WILD ROSE
Rosa woodsii

11,500 FEET

Lake Helene. Glenn Randall

INSIDER'S PICK

Lake Helene, Odessa Lake, Fern Lake

Access: Bear Lake Trailhead
Finish: Fern Lake Trailhead (free seasonal shuttle stop 0.8 miles)
Distance one-way: 8.6 miles
Access elevation: 9,475 feet
Elevation at highest destination: 10,580 feet (Lake Helene)
Finish elevation: 8,155 feet

In the Bear Lake region, a backcountry trek becomes a loop hike with a little help. Start out at one of the corridor's trailheads and emerge at another after enjoying a walk that rarely revisits any stretch of trail. Make sure there is a ride or a vehicle waiting. Better yet, take advantage of the park's free seasonal shuttle serving the entire Bear Lake Road corridor.

All that said, this exceptional backcountry experience tops many lists of favorite Rocky Mountain National Park loop hikes.

Most of the uphill work from Bear Lake is dispensed with early on. As it approaches Lake Helene, located about 0.1 miles off the main trail in the shadow of Notchtop Mountain, the now flat-to-downhill Fern Lake Trail reveals the scenic wonders of Odessa Gorge, including Grace Falls on the canyon's far wall. Soon, gorgeous Odessa Lake appears and later, hikers visit Fern Lake, Fern Falls and The Pool, all worthy stopovers. One last easy stretch of trail follows the Big Thompson River to the Fern Lake Trailhead.

> **Inside Scoop:** "A transportation tip: Park early at the Fern Lake Trailhead, ride the shuttle to Bear Lake, and hike to your car."

Dream Lake. James Frank

Nymph Lake, Dream Lake, Lake Haiyaha, Alberta Falls

Access: Bear Lake Trailhead
Finish: Glacier Gorge Trailhead (free seasonal shuttle)
Distance one-way: 6.8 miles
Access elevation: 9,475 feet
Elevation at highest destination: 10,220 feet
(Lake Haiyaha)
Finish elevation: 9,180 feet

Lake Haiyaha. James Frank

This backcountry adventure visits the park's most popular waterfall and three mountain lakes unique in their scenic beauty.

Subalpine forests shelter much of the trail walked this day, but open areas along the way offer spectacular mountain views. Each of the lakes visited is distinctive – Nymph filling with yellow-flowering pond lilies in midsummer, Dream affording its generous views of Hallett Peak, and Haiyaha tempting photographers with its boulder-strewn shoreline. After making the long walk downhill from Lake Haiyaha, hikers enjoy the exuberant cascades and cooling spray at Alberta Falls.

Inside Scoop: "In summer, there are lots of people at Bear Lake, many at Nymph and Dream, and far fewer at Lake Haiyaha."

Cub Lake, The Pool

Access: Cub Lake Trailhead
Finish: Fern Lake Trailhead
(free seasonal shuttle stop 0.8 miles)
Distance one-way: 5.2 miles

Access elevation: 8,080 feet
Elevation at highest destination: 8,620 feet
(Cub Lake)
Finish elevation: 8,155 feet

Some hikers who favor trails through the high-altitude world overlook the park's lower-elevation walks. This trip may be easier than treks across the Continental Divide, but few are as beloved.

The Cub Lake-Pool hike is a celebration of the park's diversity, showcasing mountain scenery, interesting rock formations, rushing streams dammed by beavers, forests carpeted by ferns that turn a brilliant yellow in the fall, abundant wildflowers, birds that fill the air with song and rare sightings of mountain lion prints or an itinerant moose. Cub Lake invites hikers to rest and refresh before descending to The Pool, where the Big Thompson River rushes through a granite waterpocket. The rocks surrounding The Pool are popular hiker hangouts.

Inside Scoop: "The trail visits huge, probably fallen boulders called Arch Rocks a little more than a mile from the Fern Lake Trailhead."

Fall colors near Cub Lake. Mary Ann Kressig

Albert Bierstadt's painting of Bierstadt Lake. Courtesy Buffalo Bill Historical Center, Cody, Wyo.

Sprague Lake, Glacier Basin CG

Access: Bear Lake Trailhead
Finish: Glacier Basin Campground
  (free seasonal shuttle)
Distance one-way: 4.1 miles
Access elevation: 9,475 feet
Elevation at highest destination: 9,475 feet
  (Bear Lake)
Finish elevation: 8,600 feet

This trip doesn't appear in many Rocky Mountain National Park hiking guides, but consider what it offers. Most of the hiking is on a level or downhill grade beside a mountain stream. The crowds are surprisingly thin, and the Glacier Basin scenery is grand, as are the summer wildflowers and a picnic on the shoreline at Sprague Lake. After enjoying the lake's entertaining ducks, chipmunks, ground squirrels, trailside benches and a restroom break, follow Glacier Creek to the hike's completion at Loop D in the Glacier Basin Campground.

> **Inside Scoop:** "Some pretty good fishing can be found in Glacier Creek from just below the Glacier Gorge Trailhead to the campground."

Bierstadt Lake

Access: Bear Lake Trailhead
Finish: Bierstadt Lake Trailhead
  (free seasonal shuttle)
Distance one-way: 3.4 miles
Access elevation: 9,475 feet
Destination elevation: 9,416 feet
Finish elevation: 8,850 feet

Around 1877, Albert Bierstadt painted near the shoreline of the lake now bearing his name. His creative brush captured deer wading in the chill water, autumn-tinged aspen leaves and sunshine pouring through storm clouds cloaking the peaks above. The scenes that inspired the famed artist are mostly unchanged more than a century later.

Most of the elevation gain on the way to the lake is completed in the first half mile. The trail winds across a glacial moraine through mixed forests of evergreen and aspen. After a respite on a shoreline where Bierstadt put paint to canvas, it's a scenic, sometimes hot walk down a series of steep switchbacks to the Bierstadt Lake Trailhead.

> **Inside Scoop:** "Take a map and refer to it often. Trails in the Bierstadt Lake area can be confusing. Read the map and signs carefully."

INSIDER'S PICK

Moraine Park Museum

Access: Bear Lake Road
Elevation: 8,140 feet

Moraine Park. James Frank

Sweeping westward from the sun porch at the Moraine Park Museum is an epic view of Moraine Park, a large, scenically spectacular glacial valley surrounded by forested moraines and towering mountain peaks. Visitors to the one-time resort assembly hall during the early to mid-1900s saw another picture entirely.

Moraine Park was home to a sizable settlement. Hundreds of visitors relaxed in private summer cabins or rustic resorts such as the Brinwood Hotel, Moraine Lodge and Steads Ranch, which was developed on the homestead of Abner E. Sprague. The valley hummed with summer activity, including outdoor cookouts, games of horseshoes and golf, horseback rides and square dancing. Some guests fished in the Big Thompson River or sunned themselves beside an outdoor swimming pool. Business was transacted in the post office and a small grocery store. Most of the Moraine Park structures – as well as other buildings along the Bear Lake corridor – were removed later as the National Park Service worked to restore the park to its near-natural state.

Inside Scoop: "Don't miss the interactive museum exhibits telling the story of the effects of glaciers and climate on the park."

Moraine Park Museum. James Frank

William Allen White Cabin. James Lindberg

William Allen White Cabin

Renowned Kansas journalist William Allen White purchased a cabin south of today's Moraine Park Museum in 1912. The White family later added two one-room bunkhouses and a writing cabin to the property. Sold to the National Park Service in 1972, the structures became the first buildings in the park accepted for listing on the National Register of Historic Places. Today, the main cabin provides housing for the park's artist-in-residence program.

Forest Inn

Two Rocky Mountain National Park guest lodges were not accessible by road and could be visited only on foot or horseback. One of them, Forest Inn, was located near The Pool, a granite basin in the Big Thompson River west of Moraine Park. Guests enjoyed the resort's amenities and splendid isolation until 1952.

Fern Lodge

Built by physician William Jacob Workman and completed in 1911, Fern Lodge occupied the shoreline of Fern Lake. It also was not accessible by automobile. In addition to welcoming summer visitors, the enterprise was a popular destination for winter excursions. Fern Lodge ceased opera-

tions in the late 1950s and suffered through years of vandalism and neglect before it was burned to the ground in 1976.

Hollowell Park CCC Camp

A tent camp in Hollowell Park housed workers employed by the Civilian Conservation Corps (CCC), a Depression-era work relief program. Workers were paid $1 a day to perform such tasks as construction of trails, buildings and the classic retaining walls along Trail Ridge Road.

Sprague's Lodge

Sprague's Lodge, the second Bear Lake region guest ranch developed by Abner E. Sprague, opened in 1915 and was operated successfully until 1958. The buildings are gone, but Sprague Lake, built to provide fishing for guests, remains one of Rocky Mountain National Park's most popular sites.

Bear Lake Lodge

Most visitors who stand on the Bear Lake shoreline each year think the cool subalpine forests always met the lake water unobstructed. Not so. Bear Lake once was home to a summer camp for boys and the Bear Lake Lodge, which advertised two rustic-style lodge buildings, cabins, food service and a livery.

(Above) Sprague's Lodge. Rocky Mountain National Park/Cheryl Pennington.

Alberta Falls

Area pioneer and resort owner Abner E. Sprague named this dramatic waterfall in honor of his wife.

Bear Lake

Bears are rare sightings at the lake, but early rancher Horace Ferguson saw one there, probably a black bear.

Bierstadt Lake

Its name honors noted artist Albert Bierstadt, who admired the lake during the 1870s.

Abner E. Sprague

Black Lake

Many Glacier Gorge lakes bear the names of colors, including Black, Blue and Green.

Cub Lake

Abner Sprague gave the lake this name because it's small – just a cub of a lake.

Dream Lake

This hiking destination once was known as Emerald Lake and Lake Ursula. George Barnard of the Colorado Mountain Club named it for good during a 1913 outing.

Emerald Lake

It may have been named for its distinctive greenish color.

Fern Falls

Fern Lodge proprietor William J. Workman once called this Fern Creek waterfall Lulu, the nickname of his third wife.

Fern Lake

Names given several features along Fern Creek may have been inspired by the beautiful plant.

Flattop Mountain

This mountain known for its fairly level, expansive summit formerly was called Table Top Mountain.

Lake Haiyaha

Pronounced *Hi-ya-ha,* this Arapaho Indian word means rock.

Hallett Peak

The name honors William L. Hallett, an Estes Park summer resident who came to the area in 1878 and helped form Colorado's first climbing club.

The Loch

With a clever twist, Abner Sprague used the Scottish word *loch,* meaning lake, to honor Mr. Locke, a Kansas City banker.

Mills Lake

Writer-naturalist Enos A. Mills built the rustic Longs Peak Inn at the foot of Longs Peak and championed the formation of Rocky Mountain National Park.

Moraine Park

This great valley was named for the moraines – glacially deposited accumulations of rock and earth – marking its north and south boundaries.

Nymph Lake

Once known as Lily Pad Lake and Grant Lake, the lake's permanent name was derived from *Nymphae polysepala,* the pond lilies that float on its surface.

Odessa Lake

Lodge proprietor William J. Workman had a daughter named Dessa. Odessa caught on, according to Dessa, possibly because her father "thought it more poetic."

Otis Peak

This peak was named for Boston physician Edward Osgood Otis, who climbed mountains in the Estes Park area during the 1880s.

Sky Pond

This whimsical name bestowed by Robert Sterling Yard, a conservationist and the first educational division chief for the National Park Service, is reflective of the breathtaking scenery often mirrored in the small lake's surface.

Taylor Peak

Host Abner Sprague thought highly enough of guest Albert Taylor, president of the Kansas State Normal School in Emporia, to name this prominent peak in his honor.

Timberline Falls

Robert Sterling Yard, the author of the first park information brochure, named these falls located at treeline.

Snowshoers below Hallett Peak. James Fran

Bierstadt Lake. Glenn Randall

INSIDER'S PICK

Bierstadt Lake

Access: Bear Lake Trailhead

Finish: Bierstadt Lake Trailhead or Hollowell Park Trailhead

Distance one-way: 3.4 miles (Bierstadt Lake Trailhead), 5.1 miles (Hollowell Park Trailhead)

Access elevation: 9,475 feet

Destination elevation: 9,416 feet

Finish elevation: 8,850 feet (Bierstadt Lake Trailhead), 8,380 feet (Hollowell Park Trailhead)

Winter does wondrous things to the Rocky Mountains. When cloaked in snow, close-in places feel wilder, more serene. Most visitors who make this journey on cross-country skis or snowshoes will argue that Bierstadt Moraine and the mountains towering above are even more beautiful when covered in white. (The Bear Lake Road corridor's free shuttle service doesn't operate in the winter, so trips beginning and ending at different trailheads require a ride or a vehicle waiting at the end of the trail.)

After its short, steep half-mile ascent from Bear Lake (skiers may require climbing skins), the trail becomes flat-to-downhill. For skiers, it's sometimes fast and fun. If conditions permit, head to the far side of the lake for fine mountain views. Snowshoers can descend through pine forests, naked aspen trees, steep switchbacks and breathtaking scenery to the Bierstadt Lake Trailhead. Skiers are advised to backtrack to the main trail from Bear Lake and ski out via the longer, less steep yet occasionally challenging route to Hollowell Park.

Inside Scoop: "This is one of the safest winter trips in the park, with no known avalanche potential."

Nymph, Dream & Emerald Lakes

Access: Bear Lake Trailhead
Distance one-way: 1.8 miles
Access elevation: 9,475 feet
Elevation at highest destination: 10,080 feet
(Emerald Lake)

These popular destinations host many winter visitors who follow in the boot prints of untold thousands of summer hikers. The cold months bring their unique beauty and some wilderness solitude to this popular and spectacular chain of lakes.

When frozen solid, Nymph Lake and Dream Lake tempt some skiers and snowshoers to take a shortcut across. It's always safer to walk around frozen lakes, which pose the hazards of thin ice, especially near inlets and outlets. Another 0.7 miles uphill from Dream Lake, Emerald Lake becomes diamond-like when frozen, and it offers great views of Hallett Peak, Flattop Mountain and an icy waterfall on the lake's far side.

> **Inside Scoop:** "Avalanche gear, including a small shovel and an avalanche beacon, is recommended for winter backcountry travel. Call or stop by a visitor center for the latest conditions."

Mills Lake

Access: Glacier Gorge Trailhead
Distance one-way: 2.8 miles
Access elevation: 9,180 feet
Destination elevation: 9,940 feet

Mills Lake is a favorite winter destination in Glacier Gorge, one of Rocky Mountain National Park's more scenic thoroughfares. Many skiers and snowshoers consider a trip to Mills Lake a good day's outing, although some fit, seasoned and well-equipped mountaineers push on another 2.2 miles to Black Lake.

Often swept clean by relentless winter winds, Mills Lake offers stunning views of Longs Peak. Something to consider when deciding upon a mode of travel: The route is steep in places. Skiers, who often require climbing skins for the trek uphill, regularly report nerve-wracking descents.

> **Inside Scoop:** "Anyone continuing beyond Mills Lake should have route-finding skills, as well as avalanche training and equipment."

Cub Lake

Access: Cub Lake Trailhead
Distance one-way: 2.3 miles
Access elevation: 8,080 feet
Destination elevation: 8,620 feet

A winter trek to Cub Lake can be a temporary antidote for cabin fever. Even cold, windy days on this trail may be spent in hiking boots, which feel pretty good when laced up in midwinter.

The trail often is free of snow as it skirts Moraine Park en route to Cub Creek. Snowshoes or skis may be required after the trail steepens, but hikers often are able to walk all the way to Cub Lake in the wintertime. They visit interesting boulders, a willow-fringed stream and a frozen lake backed by a photogenic view of Stones Peak.

> **Inside Scoop:** "Look for wildlife tracks in the snow along the Cub Creek streambed."